The Psychology of Rough Water

The Psychology of Rough Water

Poems by

Nancy Austin

© 2025 Nancy Austin. All rights reserved.
This material may not be reproduced in any form, published,
reprinted, recorded, performed, broadcast,
rewritten, or redistributed without
the explicit permission of Nancy Austin.
All such actions are strictly prohibited by law.

Cover design by Shay Culligan
Cover image by Blake Wisz on Unsplash
Author photo by Mia Speccio

ISBN: 978-1-63980-781-9
Library of Congress Control Number: 2025942067

Kelsay Books
502 South 1040 East, A-119
American Fork, Utah 84003
Kelsaybooks.com

*for my family, friends,
and all those who favor kindness and compassion*

Acknowledgments

Thank you to the editors of these publications in which the following poems have appeared, some in slightly different versions:

As You Were; The Military Review: "Oh Mama"
Blue Heron Review: "Shinrin-yoku (Forest Bathing)"
Bramble Literary Magazine: "Grandmas Can Dance," "Milestone Anniversary"
Eco Poetry Walk, Steven's Point, WI: "Save the Violets"
Landward: Readings of Place and Season Podcast: "500 K Cholesterol Run"
Reflections From the Center: "Power in the Hands"
Remnants of Warmth (Kelsay Books, 2016): "Of Poets and Purveyors," "WomanKind"
Silver Birch Press: "Partings," "Little Lambs"
The Thunderbird Review: "I Wake My Husband"
The Turn of the Tiller, The Spill of the Wind (Kelsay Books, 2019): "Evan on the Outside"
Ukraine: A World Anthology of Poems on War: "Empty Strollers"
Verse Virtual: "Autumn's Honorable Mention," "This One," "The Psychology of Rough Weather," "The Universe Grants Council"
The Wisconsin Poets Calendars: "My Dehydrated Neighbor," "Airbrushed," "How to Find Your Orchid"

Contents

I. Nature, Nurture

Shinrin-yoku (Forest Bathing)	15
The Golden Hour	16
What They Miss	17
This One	18
The weight of influence over a child	19
Of Poets and Purveyors	20
The Universe Grants Counsel	21
Five Hundred-Fifty K Cholesterol Run	22
Driving Spring	24
How to Find Your Rare Orchid	25
Her Superpower	26
I Wake My Husband	27
Autumn's Honorable Mention	28

II. Rough Water

A Woman Walks Alone	31
Empty Strollers	32
Power in the Hands	33
Silence Grows Monstrous Gales	34
When You Can't Kill with Kindness	35
WomanKind	36
Tomorrow's Trilogy	37
Climate of Privilege	39
Save the Violets	40
Smoking Canadian Cigarettes	41
Hyper-partisans	42
The Day After	43
The Psychology of Rough Weather	44

My dehydrated neighbor ... 45
Airbrushed ... 46

III. The Stuff

Raymond Returns ... 49
Partings ... 50
Evan on the Outside ... 52
My Grandson's Girlfriend ... 53
Oh, Mama ... 54
Ode to Em ... 55
Flo's Note to William (after William Carlos William's This Is
    Just to Say) ... 56
The Weed ... 57
Growing Friends ... 58
Finding Dad ... 59
Mom's Long-Awaited Toast ... 60
Little Lambs ... 61
Grandmas Can Dance ... 62
Our Milestone Anniversary ... 63

I.
Nature, Nurture

Shinrin-yoku (Forest Bathing)

My summer sanctuary has changed.
Moss stars that border the soggy leaf's path
are snow-dusted, the bog's boardwalk looks
briny, bobcat prints sleuth across.
I scan the bog of spent cotton grass,
tufts of white, like meadow flowers.

The boardwalk beckons, I cross over,
passing pitcher plants, bright green vessels
with blood red veins, shark-like mouths
that await prey. I step over a fallen birch branch
colonized with whimsical mushrooms,
tan polka dots on bright yellow.

I enter the open arms of this old growth forest,
its entrance dark, dank with summer's decay,
interior lit in greens and gold by rays that dapple
and dance off hemlock and pine.

The trail leads down to a clearing, a wild lake,
its periphery thick with sun-sparked trees,
russet, orange, crimson. The loons are gone,
but birdsong, now dampened by the season,
swells to ask who I am.

I hike to my talisman tree, a winter-hushed hemlock,
ancient giant whose base looks like twisted licorice,
as though a great wind twirled it, dipped it low,
laid it to rest in canopies of sister trees.

With heightened senses of shinrin-yoku
I give thanks for this dear old tree,
somehow still here, like me.

The Golden Hour

On the treetop deck, just before evening,
sounds are more endearing, closer,
carried on hot, humid air.
The loon's soft yodel from the far away bay,
a barred owl's constant question.

In the golden hour, colors more intense—
lavender petunias turn periwinkle,
geraniums—drop-dead red.
Blackbird's red-winged patches,
luminescent, dot lakeside cattails,
their calls, throaty, abrupt, now sweeter.

As the golden hour matures, light becomes
diffused and kind—softens everything.
There's a knowing—dreamy, nostalgic—
that ripens joy and gratitude, a call to just be,
like ripples on a tranquil lake that emanate
from a kayak's wake.

In the golden hour when sun is low,
the moon's in waiting. There's a feeling
time is running out, a coaxing to catch
my breath, pay attention, find my place
among these gifts.

What They Miss

grandsons pass in hall
without a nod, their heads bowed
to technology

before searing sun
bluegills feed on lake's surface
osprey dives feet first

paint chipped porch swing creaks
brushes lavender branches
lilac's spicy scent

Unfurling clouds race
above forest canopy
hermit thrush plays flute

lamp post globe reflects
stagnant rain puddle below
mosquito on moon

This One

Baby sea turtles, like tiny tanks in an army,
advance over stones, around driftwood, across sand,
as cohorts fall to attack gulls and frigates.

Ghost crabs scurry from burrows to ambush,
to snatch them up. Little leatherbacks in ancient
reptilian cadence march, hatchlings who have never

tasted salt will spend their lives at sea.
The ocean reaches out, draws them in—
to the jaws of a rockfish, a barracuda, a tiger shark—

one in a thousand survives. Ten years later this one
will emerge in moonlight on powerful limbs,
to lay her clutch of eggs.

The weight of influence over a child

is great. They watch, imitate.
Little onlookers intent on modeling.
A toddler handed his first ice cream cone freezes,
looks around the table for clues, follows his mother's
every move with concern until sugar launches his tastebuds.
If she smashed her cone on her forehead, would he follow suit?

Our grand-toddler lives near ocean, hasn't hiked north woods.
Wide-eyed in his stroller he strains upward at giant hemlocks.
Stroller wheels clickity-clack a bog's boardwalk to enter forest.
My husband steps off to examine a red-veined pitcher plant.
I warn him, for the benefit of our ward, *stay on the safety walk.*
He coaxes me and my camera into the bog, I step gingerly,
toe first to test spongy ground, arms up for balance.
Water oozes from sphagnum moss, concerned utterances
escape my mouth.

Deep in the forest I unbuckle stroller straps, lift our little guy out.
He steps toes first, arms up, slow, careful, looking for approval.
Puzzled, I remove his crocs to empty sand, but they're dry.
He continues this goofy walk.

Ah, the bog, I blurt out loud, lean down,
whisper *this* ground is hard, just like home.
With complete trust he nods, takes off down the trail.

Of Poets and Purveyors

Thunderheads billow into sculptures
of The Thinker—furrowed brows, head in hand.
Dandelions, milkweed, clover are dismissed as weeds,
their purveyor, the rusty patched bumblebee, endangered,
the meadow, a flag without its breeze.

Who decides what's a flower, what's a weed?

Poets, like dandelions, milkweed, clover,
track the sun, plant roots deep,
defy drought, backs all but broken
—with seed.

The Universe Grants Counsel

Down-hearted for days I decide
to take a winter ride.

A flash of silver hits my windshield,
startles the ice-scraper out of my hand.

A Morning Dove flips from glass to garage,
a vast, dark shadow, Coopers Hawk,

careens in after it, exits the service door.
I collect myself, tiptoe in, look around.

The dove is sheltered behind recycle bins.
Hazel eyes meet ebony eyes; we freeze.

A close call, I whisper, *but you're safe,*
back away, leave it alone.

Later, it ventures out but needs
encouragement to take leave.

I guide it with soft sweeps of mail I fetched.
After several false starts it takes flight,

lights on a snowy tree, rests a moment,
soars out of sight.

Disheartened from my own false starts,
I sigh, smile, nod, take in the lesson.

Five Hundred-Fifty K Cholesterol Run

We pack lunch, head south to the heart of Wisconsin.
Northwoods conifers, oaks, bountiful blue waterways
give way to green—open land, rolling hills, crop fields,
maples, willows, apple trees abloom in red, white, lime, pink.
Blue herons hunt water-filled roadside ditches bordering
country lanes connecting generational farms.

We roll windows down to sweet alfalfa scent, lush fields,
brilliant as only spring sprouts can be. We round corners,
gaze out at hills dotted with reddish brown and white cows,
Guernseys in various states of repose, barns, iconic red,
faded to newly painted, boasting heraldry, signature coats
of arms, quilt-like colorful broadsides.

A farmer bounces an old tractor with a manure spreader.
We wave, wrinkle noses, roll up windows.
We're on a star search, Union Star, Weyauwega Star,
any of the cheese factories found on these country lanes.
We drive down roads seeking signs to head this way
or that until the next whitewashed brick building appears,
stainless steel tanks of milk looming at its sides, *Stop!*

Pungent scent of ripening cheese wafts out the open door.
An eager man in white coat and hat catches us eying aged cheddar,
shares *something even more special,* unwraps a block of 5 years,
cubes it like a mother preens her child. He watches as crystals,
salty, potent ignite our tastebuds, explains the chemistry, switches
from lofty to lay, *flavor beads that burst on the tongue.*

We learn about Colby, created in Wisconsin, curd-like longhorn Colby, smooth Colby, Colby Jack, Colby infused with garlic, onion, smoke, dill. Cheesemakers have their own twist, he shares, Hook's Colby took the world championship in '82. We fill our bags, cheeses buttery white, yellow, orange, mild, sharp, crumbly, smooth, wedges, blocks, horns, wheels, bags of curds.

Between cheese factories we come across family meat markets, locally sourced offerings in tidy trays, butchers behind counters wait to wait on us. We sample beef and rutabaga pasties, farmer's ring sausage, ham salad on rye toast points, select from shelves stocked with baby pickled beets, corn relish, briny mushrooms.

On way home brewpubs beckon from billboards of glasses spilling suds, sandhills sleuth corn fields for seed, one foot directly in front of the other, migrating swans, snow geese—we can't tell what—congregate on lakes. We head back to our neighborhood, rustic land of pine and loons, sampling squeaky fresh cheese curds, chewy meat sticks, snippets of ham, spears of asparagus, our packed lunches abandoned in the back seat.

Driving Spring

Why does lipogram have so many vowels?

Big rig, third shift
inkish, night's pitch.
Lights blink, wind rips,
mills whir, signs whip.

First shift, night lifts,
silk hills, vivid pink
birds light, limbs sing,
mist swirls, windmills zing.

Firs drip, birch gilds
wild iris cliff's rim
mint's whiff fills ditch
rich licks, spring's riff.

How to Find Your Rare Orchid

for Mike

Lace up your boots, go to your wild place.
Look out from rocky outcrops, drop down
the loose, steep ledge into peaty fen, pay homage
to rock harlequins, pink and yellow, stop to admire
Jack-in-the Pulpit's green and brown striped hoods,
venture into delicious deciduous woods filled with
fecund soil, spot your favorite forest mushrooms:
black trumpets, bear's head tooth, chicken of the woods.

Stay clear of swamp or wet meadow; you've searched
these bogs, groves of tamaracks, black spruce.
You won't find it where you think.

Your rare orchid awaits just beyond dense trees
in the ditch of the dirt road, tall, regal queen
of humble settings, brilliant white blooms hover
like angel wings above its flashy magenta pouch.

Sit beside it, tell it your truth, leave it in peace.
On the way home find the many wonders that lie
in the ordinary. Tack this poem to a tree.

Her Superpower

for Jan

The human race has only one effective weapon and that is laughter.
—Mark Twain

Set in motion she bobs up and down, a mini jack hammer,
sputters, hisses like an engine, coolant leaking,
overheated, breakdown eminent, and then—the snorts.
No abashed, unexpected escapee, but full-frontal serial snorts,
delivered by design, perfected with age.

Conference goers' coffee cups freeze in mid-air,
conversations quit, heads fly back with her next backfire,
a rebound off the crowd's virulent laughter that radiates
from ground zero like a stadium wave, reaches critical mass
where extremities flail, tears flow, milk bubbles from a nose,
women over sixty Kegel and dash, the crowd—
breathless, bonded, endorphin-enriched.

I Wake My Husband

A lone wolf howls in the wood's vast darkness,
the chug-chug-chug of a Flight for Life copter
skims trees along its route above Bearskin trail.
Prayers float up from cabins, homes, beds.

Ten o'clock news tells of an epic geomagnetic storm.
We join hands, pad down the hill in slippers and robes.
Eyes adjust, knees creak to the lake clearing where
Aurora pirouettes across sky.

White beams like footlights scan the horizon,
brighten a backdrop of magenta swirls and arcs.
Violet, florescent green, electric pink, ruby red spread
like watercolor on wet canvas above lake's moon wake.

We stand in pjs, wordless, our heads to the stars.
The curtain falls, I offer thanks, check elusive Aurora
off my bucket list. A last beam lights the sky as if
to carry Rumi's words:

Beautiful days do not come to you,
You must walk towards them.

Autumn's Honorable Mention

Wind works its way through forest's dazzling display,
sweeps up a blaze of kaleidoscope leaves.
Like tamaracks I'm still green, do not stand out,
but am blessed with blue jays, squirrels, chickadees.

In my autumn I too will amaze, you will see.
But not when leaves are golden, scarlet, starlit.
Slow, steady, late as usual, I'll come to light
like tamaracks aglow against leafless trunks.

II.
Rough Water

A Woman Walks Alone

Jack pines—crooked, craggy trunks, knobby branches,
leafless limbs that arch downward like alien arms
with elongated hands, curved claws.

I never noticed them in full foliage among
oaks and aspen, and coax myself, *walk on.*
A hermit thrush calls from deep in the forest,
flute-like, ethereal—a harbinger?

I focus on the happy *hank, hank, hank* of a nuthatch,
the unfolding of spring trilliums, marsh marigolds.
Damp-earth breezes lift and perfume my hair.
I reach the long stretch with no cabins, a quiet road
along forest, and venture out, but worry encroaches—
a mountain lion or sentinel wolf could be pacing me.

I hear wind in trees—no—an approaching car,
think of the woman who went missing on Bearskin Trail.
I chide my racing heart, round the corner,
meet a doe munching on roadside grass.
Skittish at the motor's sound, she periscopes her ears,
twitches her tail, stomps her hoof, holds her ground.

The car passes, I collect myself, carry on.

Empty Strollers

Galyna flees with her husband, grandkids
in tow—a two-year old, a baby still nursing.
They're stopped at a checkpoint, her husband
convinced to stay, to fight.

She continues to herd the toddler,
grandbaby in a sling, formula the infant balks at,
tins of sardines their only food. Lining Poland's
border are empty strollers for the taking.

Galyna lowers the children into one.
Her thoughts turn to her husband, his unfilled
blood pressure meds, her daughter, son-in-law
under the rubble of their leveled high rise.

The Polish women receive Galyna with hugs,
change the baby, feed them, direct them to rest.
Safe in this tent community, Galena's numbness
thick and insulating as the gifted Polish blankets.

The empty strollers, the look in the women's eyes
as they lift her little ones, the endearment of *siostra*
while they wash a week's worth of grime from her face
finally affords Galyna the luxury of tears.

Power in the Hands

What kind of hands target maternity wards,
bomb hospitals, buildings marked "children" in Russian?
Atrocities at the hands of a man after power.

A reporter in a food shelter interviews workers
feeding hundreds per day. He stops Bohdana,
a Ukrainian kitchen worker, to ask,
*Is this your way of fighting? Such a smile
on your face in the middle of a war.*

Bombs whistle, buildings tremble, sirens sound.
Her hands on his arm, she tells him in broken English,
It is my power. My weapons are spoons and forks.

Dear Bohdana, your name translates
to "God-gift." *Power to you.*

Silence Grows Monstrous Gales

When we lookout from our windows, safe, sun shining bright,
it's hard to think of all the people for whom peace is denied.
Parents sift through silt and rubble, wounded children cry,
power seeking hate agendas fuel chaos worldwide.

It's hard to think of all the people for whom peace is denied.
When leaders' only motivation is to stay in power,
power-seeking hate agendas fuel chaos worldwide,
altruism is circumvented, intimidation cowers.

When leaders only motivation is to stay in power,
it's hard to stand up to the hostile, to call out what's not right,
altruism is circumvented, intimidation cowers,
when it comes to speaking up, we find our tongues are tied.

It's hard to stand up to the hostile, to call out what's not right.
Parents sift through silt and rubble, wounded children cry,
when it comes to speaking up, we find our tongues are tied
when we look out from our windows, safe, sun shining bright.

When You Can't Kill with Kindness

The heartless hunter keen to the doe
he's filled his tag but she's deep in snow,
the whippoorwill cries out in the night
her haunting voice denied in light.

He's filled his tag but she's deep in snow.
Those who take and take want more and more,
her haunting voice denied in light,
they berate and belittle those they claim to care for.

Those who take and take want more and more,
they charm to pull you in, use you like a tool,
berate and belittle those they claim to care for,
leverage love and value their things above you.

They charm to pull you in, use you like a tool.
I'm told that being kind has its own authority,
they leverage love and value their things above you,
kindness is fuel for the narcissist.

I'm told that being kind has its own authority,
you can't kill heartless with kindness,
kindness is fuel for the narcissist,
the heartless hunter keen to the doe.

WomanKind

Ferocity has her, empty-handed swordfighter,
in a choke hold. Her blocking techniques—
sweeping low block, rising palm block,
hands together block belie the percussive
racing rhythm of an unarmed heart.

For years she's bypassed battle, for years
she has been battered as she masters this deadly dance
of self-defense in grace, solidarity and strength.
Pushed to the precipice she will circle you
with a flurry of flying jump kicks, knee strikes,
a scissors strike close to the spleen, a stomp
just short of your heart. Spared and supine,
she'll cover you with a coat of humility
as you slither away.

Sated, safe, she'll take leave in stillness
to breathe back what was lost, seek caritas,
steel herself for the next round with Kipling's tale
of the mongoose who dodges and dances outside
the cobra's deadly strike, seemingly afraid,
secretly skilled. Unbeknownst to the cobra,
the mongoose is resistant to its venom.

For years she's bypassed battle, for years
she has been battered, slashes here, wounds there,
have rendered her immune.
Some see her olive branch as a failing,
her, a frail-ing, but know this:
in this conceivably deadly dance,
she is the mongoose.

Tomorrow's Trilogy

I.

this time he brings phlox
from Tomorrow River's edge
purple as her eye

II.

Wild daisies, like the ones he handed her after his last outburst, dot sedges along the Tomorrow River. She pulls her cherry red kayak through mossy water, through the sway of purple pickerel near shore. He grabs the kayak, her eyes directed to her bruised wrist. Feathery willow fingers stir up stagnant water, bleached barn looms over haybales wound tight as her nerves. They skirt the field's edge, climb the bluff, take their places in two empty chairs overlooking the highway.

golden aspen leaves
fall from branch like confetti
a shrike is exposed

III.

The Tomorrow River snakes around groves
of maple, ash, an occasional lone elm,
carves a path below two empty chairs,
silhouettes on a bluff above the highway.
She climbs the hill, flooded with flashbacks.
How his praise, charm, flattery had turned,
his clenched fist more erratic, opposition severe.

If she craved beef, he insisted on chicken,
if she offered an opinion, he opined the opposite.
If a sign said stop, he would go, if an arrow
pointed right he was determined to go left.
She learned to state the reverse of what she wanted,
avoided travel by insisting on riding along.

In spring she climbs the summit, folds his empty chair,
feels kinship with the valley's verdant unfurling,
turns her head toward a sign the city erected.
Looming above the highway, not far from
where he rolled his truck, the new billboard,
Buckle Up and Slow Down.

Climate of Privilege

Scientists are silenced,
clean energy, car emissions,
protections for threatened species
fodder for disinformation.

Our carbon footprints thunderous
in developing countries where
drought, starvation begets violence.
We turn away families that flee,

snuggle in silk sheets while our excess
melts Arctic ice sheets, super storms sweep
away islands, survivors succumb to foul water,
hospitals languish without power.

Now Paradise has burned, LA fires apocalyptic.
We gasp from afar, then acclimate in luxury.
What will it take to act? All our comforts fading
away like a whistle on a runaway train?

Save the Violets

Violets are flourishes to some, fan-shaped petals
to bejewel a wedding cake, a flirty elixir dabbed
on wrists, behind the ears.

Violets are weeds to others, delicate
blue petals belie hearty rhizomes
that self-seed with abandon.

Violets are lifelines to fritillary butterflies,
the only plants the Silver-washed, the Dark Green,
the Great Spangled lay eggs on to feed their caterpillars.

They hatch, bask on sun-soaked heart-shaped leaves,
feast, then winter in violet's dried, curled up leaves,
a haven for hibernation.

Without violets there would be no sips of nectar
in springtime, no silver-spangled underwings
to pollinate sunny glades, native wildflowers.

Smoking Canadian Cigarettes

My husband, back from the boat ride I declined,
feels greasy, antsy, a sooty taste in his mouth.
The eerie sun, nuclear orange, overtaken
again and again by smokey haze.

My sister has asthma, keeps anxiety at bay
with little luxuries—frothed coffee, good books,
unhurried brushstrokes of indigo, violet, sienna
on stark white canvas.

I call out *meals on wheels* to a spry client, no response.
Blanket held tight she's laid out in her recliner,
answers my puzzlement with *my lungs have issues,*
then cries—yesterday she thought she would die.

The furnace fan recirculates air through a MERV 13,
our home tightly sealed against Canadian plumes.
Stuck inside, my restless legs long to scissor kick,
arms to slice through clear waters of Sand Lake.

News informs us Milwaukee's air is the worst on earth,
Chicago's skyline not visible north of Diversey Avenue,
dangerous particulates can enter lungs, blood, heart—
prolonged exposure like smoking a pack a day.

Hyper-partisans

choose one thing to subsist on—
like cheesecake or cabbage, each alone, equally bad.

Team Cheesecake's rich, 900 calories a slice, days dawn decadent.
Eight slices later, food-drunk in the afternoon, the team can't rouse

from long naps, sugar-dizzy, lumber onto scales, lament the gain,
distribute the blame for fatty livers, triple bi-passes, lethargy.

Team Cabbage revels in nutrients, fiber, 300 calories per head.
They flaunt renewed energy, work out, feel fit, become lean.

Weakness sets in, they ease onto the scale, startled at their loss.
Clavicles protrude, clothes slide off, can't make it up the stairs.

The Day After

I sit on my porch, face in hands.
Frost has finished all flowers, foliage.
Colorful leaves have fallen, rusty, crisp;
barren trees shiver, songbirds gone.
My eyes settle on shriveled daffodils.

Bell Songs, Poet's Daffodils, Pink Parasols
long ago delivered across ocean took hold
like a fresh, bright idea, spread across land.
Some deemed them delicate, yet every year
they defy hard ground, emerge at winter's end.
Hardy in heat, pelting rain and hail, ever ready
to stand back up and wave a welcome to sky, earth,
and all of us in-between, ambassador of new beginnings.
Yellow on yellow, white on yellow, salmon pink trumpets
herald hope, usher in blooms of all kinds, all colors,
future generations stored in sturdy bulbs, like wombs.

Biting winds a harbinger, I pull my jacket close,
refuse to imagine a world without daffodils.

The Psychology of Rough Weather

Rain pummels the lake's lily pads
into a frenzy of wobbles and whirls,
starry blooms lurch in anxious water.

Hummingbirds duel like fighter jets
for feeders beneath dripping eaves,
lilacs scatter in sleet, torrential rain.

In this deluge I must remember
lily pads are tethered to roots,
lilacs go dormant, hummingbirds fly
over endless ocean, all to return
in spring.

My dehydrated neighbor

leans in, whispers, *those aren't her grandkids,*
she married in, that blood is thicker than water.

Blood *is* thicker than water, I counsel.
It coagulates, leaves nasty stains when exposed.
Water connects. Shapes air, clouds, sea, us.
Water is life's solvent. It doesn't disappear,
but evaporates to atmosphere to moisten air
that doesn't care with whom it's shared—
eight billion sets of lungs made mostly of water
that flows cell to cell to power our brains,
hydrate our hearts.

A neighbor tells me blood is thicker than water,
I reply we are mostly water, hand her a glass.

Airbrushed

> *. . . overly perfected beauty images can lead to body dissatisfaction, depression, anxiety and eating disorders in girls and women.*
> —Renee Engeln, Washington Post

She sprayed Windex, scrubbed,
squeegeed, toweled, stood back,
scrutinized, buffed remaining streaks,
even used the newspaper trick.

Why, she wanted to know,
can glass that looks pristine,
so cleverly cleaned, never stand up
to the rays of morning sun?

III.
The Stuff

Raymond Returns

for Mary

A Green Darner dragonfly perches
on the frayed cord of her hummingbird feeder.
Sunlit, luminescent, he lets her approach.

His back leg is tangled in a thread.
Sun-spotted, wrinkled hands tremble
it free with a mother's feather-touch.

The next day it lights on her arm.
She calls him by name, tells him
how clever to get my attention,
though she knew it was him
by the dart and dance of dragonflies
that ushered him in, Raymond humming
as always, pack of carousing cohorts in tow.

Partings

Part I: My Grown Daughter Asks About Her Grandma

Anxious to share my news, I hurried through the airport,
hand on my abdomen, new life inside that was you
—six months to go.
Anxious to share her news, wet eyes, long embrace,
hand on her abdomen, new life inside, pancreatic cancer
—six months to go.

Part II: Familial Rain

Mom's glossy-green schefflera bounces in the breeze
like her once-full head of auburn hair.
She tells me it's an epiphyte, a plant supported
by another, taking sustenance from air, from rain.
Her mottled hands palm the brown lesions
that have taken over its umbrella-like leaves.
Once these spots form there's little that can be done,
she counsels in softest voice, eyes moist, fixed on mine.
They both begin to die as my daughter grows inside.
I take a cutting from the last healthy stem,
store her stone ware planter in the garage.
The cutting from its mother plant statuesque,
its leaflets, dancing stars in the corner window breeze.

Mom, grandma, aunt, uncle die midway through
their lives, as does my commemorative plant,
consumed by malignant spots.
Decades later a cousin dies.
I retrieve mom's stoneware pot,
place a new schefflera in the corner window
to glean the last of the late afternoon sun.
Together we lean into the light,
take sustenance in the sweet scent
that hangs in the air just before
the uneasy echo of familial rain.

Evan on the Outside

Morning sickness day and night, my daughter
can't keep food down, loses weight.
Medical issues pile up like dirty laundry:
gestational diabetes, low iron, low B-6.
Smooth sailing is surely ahead I tell her,
but her thyroid crashes, her liver enlarges,
ankles so swollen a finger push leaves a pit.

We arrive the eve of delivery, wiggle my mother's
ring onto her once slender pinky for good luck,
kiss her forehead, hug her husband, send them forth.
We cheer news of Evan's arrival, head down the hall
where a nervous nurse catches up, implores us to wait.
A rapid response team hurries into her room.

Her blood pressure soars, liver, kidney labs spike,
platelets plunge, a magnesium drip staves off seizures
at the price of delirium, nausea, muscle contractions.
Her husband places ice packs on her fiery skin,
nurses pump and dump her milk, dried, cracked
lips whisper *Mama, am I ok?*

A week later we huddle in their sun-dappled den,
white walls waiting to be painted seafoam green.
Evan suckles at full breasts, opens his eyes.
We trace his tiny digits, cup his little feet.
He is mellow; he is lovely.
I lean into my daughter's ear to say,
Evan on the inside, a perfect storm.
Evan on the outside—perfect.

My Grandson's Girlfriend

bolts up the hill, asks for cardboard
to slip under a mouse on its back
trying to right itself in cold firepit ash.
She thinks it fell from an owl's talons,

feels it should die with dignity under
the bushes, implores us to hurry.
She slides the mouse onto paper, moves it
to tag alders where it rallies, nibbles on grass.

Later I find them dunking buckets into the lake
to revive our wilted, sun-parched saplings.
She coaxes our grandson to recycle. On kayaks,
she alerts a motorist of loon babies just ahead.

At dinner she shares her passions and peeves,
as quick with retort as she is with support.
I pass the crystal cut salad cruet, her reflection
dancing in facets of honey and vinegar.

Oh, Mama

An old man in a World War II cap dozed, front row
of our poetry reading, reminded me of my father,
whose eyes often closed this time of evening in sleep,
perhaps in remembrance of soldiers returning
from the Bataan death march—starved, skeletal men.

My final line, *Oh, Mama,* woke this man with a start.
Open mic began, his voice broke as he read a poem
to his deceased wife, plain spoken, steeped in devotion.

But it was his second poem: the battlefield pock-marked
with craters, he struggles to take cover over and around
bodies, hears a cry, kneels to take the soldier's hand,
leans in to hear his last words, *Oh, Mama.*

Ode to Em

Oh Em—
ily, Mother of the Em Dash—
no pregnant pause for you—
yet—Proliferation.

Your tiny offspring
gave us a space to breathe
in Cramped Quarters—
stillness—suspense
tension—a turn—
a lull—to allow
Enormity in.

Flo's Note to William (after William Carlos William's This Is Just to Say)

I have taken
your mustang
tucked in
the garage

and which
you were probably
saving
forever

Forgive me
it drives delicious
so fast
and so far

The Weed

She's suspicious of its over-eager presence,
how it sways out of step, bumps other blossoms.
He thinks it a seed of tall phlox he is enchanted by,
forbids her to pull it.

He dares her to call it a weed.
It takes over, cagey, off center.
At two feet it sprouts a purple tassel.
She apologizes, fertilizes, welcomes.

It grows woody, spans an army of underlings.
She glares from vantage points until one afternoon
sees his fist around the dangling dissident, sod-like
chunk of unearthed marigolds woven into its base.

He gets on his knees, dissects the soil,
extracts each marigold, removes rebel shoots.
Beefy fingers replant, tuck, mend the border,
return the intruder to the woods.

Growing Friends

My new neighbor, potential winter comrade,
comes for tea, consults on my anemic cactus,
singular snake whose spikey leaves flopped over
this past sunless, snowless season.

I gift her a succulent, crazy riot of tangled,
tubular strands I've named Bad Hair Day.
She offers a section of her prized jasmine,
also stressed this dark winter, in need of a repot.

Spring sun pours into her potting shed, a sharp
contrast to her new home, memorial to her thrifty
father with its leftover lumber, pallets, broken window
panes he taped together.

She digs through pots nestled like Russian dolls,
assures the jasmine, *this is as bad as it gets,*
whacks its bottom, eases it out, pries choice
sections apart, gathers them into a bouquet.

She positions it just so in my pot, props it with *rock buddies,*
sifts in fertilizer, waters a bit at a time, gives it a name.
I note this departure from my method of dump, dig, plant,
vow to cultivate two new friends: plant and plant whisperer.

Finding Dad

At ninety-nine Dad lives in the moment,
and when that moment
      is gone
he lands in the next, happy to see us.

We load his fork, coax him to take a bite, a sip.
Dementia chisels away his engaging essence,
his wit, dry humor, loquacious vocabulary,
save a few sentences he repeats over and over.

But it's in his familiar smile when he sees us
that we find him, how he somehow remembers
our names, as if, consummate careful planner,
he implored God to spare him this one grace.

Dad, ask the same question a thousand times
and we'll answer each as though it were the first.

On his last day, eyes closed before slipping
into unconsciousness, he mutters a phrase
to us again and again, *Goodbye, good luck,
I love you.*

Mom's Long-Awaited Toast

He luffs his mainsail at port, steps off,
surprised how spry, how sturdy his feet.
He celebrates deep and effortless breath,
air scented of her peonies, moss roses.
He follows the floral aisle, sits by her side.

Remembering hunger after her sojourn decades before,
she's prepared his favorites: eggplant parmesan,
Italian sausages glistening with peppers and onions.
She grins, slides him a thick slice of her cinnamon
apple pie—it's been days since he's eaten.

He raises his Merlot, they lean in, intertwine arms,
sip from each other's glass as they had done every
Sunday evening. She chides him about landing his boat
at the wrong dock, something he did when teaching us
to sail, something we all teased him about over the years.
His laughter, her playfulness, their unbreakable bond
carries down the lineage as they watch their children,
grandchildren and great grandchildren from afar.
They clink glasses, utter *Family Is Everything,*
a toast as warm and familiar as their favorite red wine.

Little Lambs

Eyes glazed, overtired he ambles over, leans against
my chair, worn blankey in hand, thumb in mouth.

I swoop him up, wait for a busy boy protest but he submits.
At four his arms, legs sprawl over armrests. We rock.

I sing melodies sung to him when he was a wee baby,
songs I sang to all my grandkids to soothe colic,

colds, crankiness, skinned knees, the same ones
I sang to my son, my daughter, from our family's

Rogers and Hammerstein book, *The Sound of Music,
South Pacific, Oklahoma, Cinderella.*

I croon folk tunes of my youth taught at day camps:
Life of a Voyager, Barges, Dona, Dona, its mournful minor key.

Lullabies, nursery rhymes, Gershwin's Summertime,
time-honored tunes echo out to generations lost, if listening.

I sing like it's the last time I'm granted this gift—
our littlest grandson is growing up.

Eyes to the ceiling he listens, conjures up a *calf
with a mournful eye*, Mary's errant little lamb.

Many times I've pondered all I might have done in my life
with more time, more resources, more courage.

But here in this magical moment of music and snuggles,
his hand in mine, *this* the stuff to live for.

Grandmas Can Dance

Alexa, play dance music, I instruct, emulate Uma
in *Pulp Fiction,* sweep two fingers over each eye,
shift my weight from one stocking foot to the other
in The Twist, plug my nose, sink, do The Swim.

The littlest catches on, mutters *Wiggle, wiggle, wiggle,*
sways his hips, throws his chubby toddler arms up and down.
Our teen, mouth agape, stares, then gyrates like a snake,
morphs into a robot. The ten-year-old does the Floss.

Grandpa rouses from the next room, demands the Hot Dog song
from Mickie Mouse, gallops in, nails Goofy's dimwitted dance.
Our 3-year-old, always eager to join the clan, commands in pixie
voice, *'Lexa, play I'm a Little Teapot,* shouting his favorite line
short and stout. After collecting ourselves, we align in solidarity,
all handles and spouts.

Our Milestone Anniversary

Tall white spruce throw reflections on the stagnant Peshtigo River,
a light breeze sets them to shimmer in rippled, slate-colored water.
Red-headed woodpeckers pierce morning stillness, call *wait, wait.*

Nuthatches, phoebes answer. We watch bits of blue break through
murky skies from the deck of a rented condo, otter heads pop out
of water, catch a brief sunray, greet one another, then part.

Intermittent mist, the return of kids to school assure us
a vast reservoir to ourselves, save a sprinkling of fishing boats.
To the south, sweltering heat, but for us, a perfect seventy-two.

We motor the expanse, duck into channels, peer at fish in tannin-
stained water, beach our boat, break out sandwiches of pulled pork,
coleslaw on Hawaiian rolls. Watermelon runs down our chins.

High above hundreds of night hawks appear, long wings flit, beaks
point south, a sign of season's end, time to take stock of this year's
blessings, hardships, the passing of yet another summer's warmth.

Water boatmen skim the calm river in spry, erratic motion
reminiscent of our youth. We putt along past blue herons tucked in
tight to shore, our long, slow wake gathers a lifetime of memories.

About the Author

Nancy Austin holds a master's in psychology and ran a Community Support Program for individuals with mental illness for many years. She retired in the Northwoods of Wisconsin where she relishes time to write, in awe of the regenerative powers of nature, its metaphors and lessons. She serves as the Northwest Region Vice President of the Wisconsin Fellowship of Poets (WFOP) and in her free time dabbles in music.

A Pushcart Prize nominated poet, she has been published in various journals and has several poetry collections, *Remnants of Warmth* (Kelsay Books, 2016), *The Turn of the Tiller, The Spill of the Wind* (Kelsay Books, 2019), and *Something Novel Came in Spring* (Water's Edge Press, 2021).

Find her in the woods, on a boat,
enjoying her five grandsons, or at:
nancyaustinauthor.com

www.ingramcontent.com/pod-product-compliance
Lightning Source LLC
Chambersburg PA
CBHW030914170426
43193CB00009BA/849